SOCIAL PROGRESS AND SUSTAINABILITY

Shelter • Safety • Literacy • Health • Freedom • Environment

CENTRAL AMERICA AND THE CARIBBEAN

Foreword by **Michael Green,**
Executive Director, Social Progress Imperative

By Judy Boyd

SOCIAL PROGRESS AND SUSTAINABILITY

THE SERIES:

AFRICA: NORTHERN AND EASTERN

AFRICA: MIDDLE, WESTERN, AND SOUTHERN

EAST ASIA AND THE PACIFIC

EUROPE

EURASIA

NEAR EAST

SOUTH AND CENTRAL ASIA

NORTH AMERICA

CENTRAL AMERICA AND THE CARIBBEAN

SOUTH AMERICA

SOCIAL PROGRESS AND SUSTAINABILITY

Shelter • Safety • Literacy • Health • Freedom • Environment

CENTRAL AMERICA AND THE CARIBBEAN

Judy Boyd

Foreword by
Michael Green
Executive Director, Social Progress Imperative

MASON CREST

Mason Crest
450 Parkway Drive, Suite D
Broomall, PA 19008
www.masoncrest.com

RAP 3 2401 00894 408 6

Printed and bound in the United States of America

First printing
9 8 7 6 5 4 3 2 1

Series ISBN: 978-1-4222-3490-7
Hardcover ISBN: 978-1-4222-3493-8
ebook ISBN: 978-1-4222-8388-2

Library of Congress Cataloging-in-Publication Data

Names: Boyd, Judy, 1950– author.
Title: Central America and the Caribbean/by Judy Boyd; foreword by Michael Green, executive director, Social Progress Imperative.
Description: Broomall, PA : Mason Crest, [2017] | Series: Social progress and sustainability | Includes index.
Identifiers: LCCN 2016007612| ISBN 9781422234938 (hardback) | ISBN 9781422234907 (series) | ISBN 9781422283882 (ebook)
Subjects: LCSH: Social indicators—Central America—Juvenile literature. | Social indicators—Caribbean Area—Juvenile literature. | Central America—Social conditions—Juvenile literature. | Central America—Economic conditions—Juvenile literature. | Caribbean Area—Social conditions—Juvenile literature. | Caribbean Area—Economic conditions—Juvenile literature.
Classification: LCC HN122.7 .B69 2017 | DDC 306.09728—dc23
LC record available at http://lccn.loc.gov/2016007612

Developed and Produced by Print Matters Productions, Inc. (www.printmattersinc.com)

Project Editor: David Andrews
Design: Bill Madrid, Madrid Design
Copy Editor: Laura Daly

CONTENTS

YA
306.69728
BOY

Foreword: Social Progress around the Globe by Michael Green **........** 6

Introduction: Social Progress in Central America and
the Caribbean **...** 11

1 Basic Human Needs 15

2 Foundations of Well-being.........................31

3 Opportunity..47

**4 Central American and Caribbean Countries
at a Glance 65**

Conclusion **...** 72

Glossary **..** 75

Index **...** 78

Resources **..** 79

KEY ICONS TO LOOK FOR:

 Text-Dependent Questions: These questions send readers back to the text for more careful attention to the evidence presented there.

 Words to Understand: These words with their easy-to-understand definitions will increase readers' understanding of the text while building vocabulary skills.

 Series Glossary of Key Terms: This back-of-the-book glossary contains terminology used throughout this series. Words found here increase readers' ability to read and comprehend higher-level books and articles in this field.

 Research Projects: Readers are pointed toward areas of further inquiry connected to each chapter. Suggestions are provided for projects that encourage deeper research and analysis.

 Sidebars: This boxed material within the main text allows readers to build knowledge, gain insights, explore possibilities, and broaden their perspectives by weaving together additional information to provide realistic and holistic perspectives.

SOCIAL PROGRESS AROUND THE GLOBE

Michael Green

How do you measure the success of a country? It's not as easy as you might think.

Americans are used to thinking of their country as the best in the world, but what does "best" actually mean? For a long time, the United States performed better than any other country in terms of the sheer size of its economy, and bigger was considered better. Yet China caught up with the United States in 2014 and now has a larger overall economy.

What about average wealth? The United States does far better than China here but not as well as several countries in Europe and the Middle East.

Most of us would like to be richer, but is money really what we care about? Is wealth really how we want to measure the success of countries—or cities, neighborhoods, families, and individuals? Would you really want to be rich if it meant not having access to the World Wide Web, or suffering a painful disease, or not being safe when you walked near your home?

Using money to compare societies has a long history, including the invention in the 1930s of an economic measurement called gross domestic product (GDP). Basically, GDP for the United States "measures the output of goods and services produced by labor and property located within the U.S. during a given time period." The concept of GDP was actually created by the economist Simon Kuznets for use by the federal government. Using measures like GDP to guide national economic policies helped pull the United States out of the Great Depression and helped Europe and Japan recover after World War II. As they say in business school, if you can measure it, you can manage it.

Many positive activities contribute to GDP, such as

- Building schools and roads
- Growing crops and raising livestock
- Providing medical care

More and more experts, however, are seeing that we may need another way to measure the success of a nation.

Other kinds of activities increase a country's GDP, but are these signs that a country is moving in a positive direction?

- Building and maintaining larger prisons for more inmates
- Cleaning up after hurricanes or other natural disasters
- Buying alcohol and illegal drugs
- Maintaining ecologically unsustainable use of water, harvesting of trees, or catching of fish

GDP also does not address inequality. A few people could become extraordinarily wealthy, while the rest of a country is plunged into poverty and hunger, but this wouldn't be reflected in the GDP.

In the turbulent 1960s, Robert F. Kennedy, the attorney general of the United States and brother of President John F. Kennedy, famously said of GDP during a 1968 address to students at the University of Kansas: "It counts napalm and counts nuclear warheads and armored cars for the police to fight the riots in our cities ... [but] the gross national product does not allow for the health of our children.... [I]t measures everything in short, except that which makes life worthwhile."

For countries like the United States that already have large or strong economies, it is not clear that simply making the economy larger will improve human welfare. Developed countries struggle with issues like obesity, diabetes, crime, and environmental challenges. Increasingly, even poorer countries are struggling with these same issues.

Noting the difficulties that many countries experience as they grow wealthier (such as increased crime and obesity), people around the world have begun to wonder: What if we measure the things we really care about directly, rather than assuming that greater GDP will mean improvement in everything we care about? Is that even possible?

The good news is that it is. There is a new way to think about prosperity, one that does not depend on measuring economic activity using traditional tools like GDP.

Advocates of the "Beyond GDP" movement, people ranging from university professors to leaders of businesses, from politicians to religious leaders, are calling for more attention to directly measuring things we all care about, such as hunger, homelessness, disease, and unsafe water.

One of the new tools that has been developed is called the Social Progress Index (SPI), and it is the data from this index that is featured in this series of books, Social Progress and Sustainability.

The SPI has been created to measure and advance social progress outcomes at a fine level of detail in communities of different sizes and at different levels of wealth. This means that we can compare the performance of very different countries using one standard set of measurements, to get a sense of how well different countries perform compared to each other. The index measures how the different parts of society, including governments, businesses, not-for-profits, social entrepreneurs, universities, and colleges, work together to improve human welfare. Similarly, it does not strictly measure the actions taken in a particular place. Instead, it measures the outcomes in a place.

The SPI begins by defining what it means to be a good society, structured around three fundamental themes:

- Do people have the basic needs for survival: food, water, shelter, and safety?
- Do people have the building blocks of a better future: education, information, health, and sustainable ecosystems?

- Do people have a chance to fulfill their dreams and aspirations by having rights and freedom of choice, without discrimination, with access to the cutting edge of human knowledge?

The Social Progress Index is published each year, using the best available data for all the countries covered. You can explore the data on our website at http://socialprogressimperative.org. The data for this series of books is from our 2015 index, which covered 133 countries. Countries that do not appear in the 2015 index did not have the right data available to be included.

A few examples will help illustrate how overall Social Progress Index scores compare to measures of economic productivity (for example, GDP per capita), and also how countries can differ on specific lenses of social performance.

- The United States (6th for GDP per capita, 16th for SPI overall) ranks 6th for Shelter but 68th in Health and Wellness, because of factors such as obesity and death from heart disease.
- South Africa (62nd for GDP per capita, 63rd for SPI) ranks 44th in Access to Information and Communications but only 114th in Health and Wellness, because of factors such as relatively short life expectancy and obesity.
- India (93rd for GDP per capita, 101st for SPI) ranks 70th in Personal Rights but only 128th in Tolerance and Inclusion, because of factors such as low tolerance for different religions and low tolerance for homosexuals.
- China (66th for GDP per capita, 92nd for SPI) ranks 58th in Shelter but 84th in Water and Sanitation, because of factors such as access to piped water.
- Brazil (55th for GDP per capita, 42nd for SPI) ranks 61st in Nutrition and Basic Medical Care but only 122nd in Personal Safety, because of factors such as a high homicide rate.

The Social Progress Index focuses on outcomes. Politicians can boast that the government has spent millions on feeding the hungry; the SPI measures how well fed people really are. Businesses can boast investing money in their operations or how many hours their employees have volunteered in the community; the SPI measures actual literacy rates and access to the Internet. Legislators and administrators might focus on how much a country spends on health care; the SPI measures how long and how healthily people live. The index doesn't measure whether countries have passed laws against discrimination; it measures whether people experience discrimination. And so on.

- What if your family measured its success only by the amount of money it brought in but ignored the health and education of members of the family?
- What if a neighborhood focused only on the happiness of the majority while discriminating against one family because they were different?
- What if a country focused on building fast cars but was unable to provide clean water and air?

The Social Progress Index can also be adapted to measure human well-being in areas smaller than a whole country.

- A Social Progress Index for the Amazon region of Brazil, home to 24 million people and covering one of the world's most precious environmental assets, shows how 800 different municipalities compare. A map of that region shows where needs are greatest and is informing a development strategy for the region that balances the interests of people and the planet. Nonprofits, businesses, and governments in Brazil are now using this data to improve the lives of the people living in the Amazon region.
- The European Commission—the governmental body that manages the European Union—is using the Social Progress Index to compare the performance of multiple regions in each of 28 countries and to inform development strategies.
- We envision a future where the Social Progress Index will be used by communities of different sizes around the world to measure how well they are performing and to help guide governments, businesses, and nonprofits to make better choices about what they focus on improving, including learning lessons from other communities of similar size and wealth that may be performing better on some fronts. Even in the United States subnational social progress indexes are underway to help direct equitable growth for communities.

The Social Progress Index is intended to be used along with economic measurements such as GDP, which have been effective in guiding decisions that have lifted hundreds of millions of people out of abject poverty. But it is designed to let countries go even further, not just making economies larger but helping them devote resources to where they will improve social progress the most. The vision of my organization, the Social Progress Imperative, which created the Social Progress Index, is that in the future the Social Progress Index will be considered alongside GDP when people make decisions about how to invest money and time.

Imagine if we could measure what charities and volunteers really contribute to our societies. Imagine if businesses competed based on their whole contribution to society—not just economic, but social and environmental. Imagine if our politicians were held accountable for how much they made people's lives better, in real, tangible ways. Imagine if everyone, everywhere, woke up thinking about how their community performed on social progress and about what they could do to make it better.

Note on Text:
While Michael Green wrote the foreword and data is from the 2015 Social Progress Index, the rest of the text is not by Michael Green or the Social Progress Imperative.

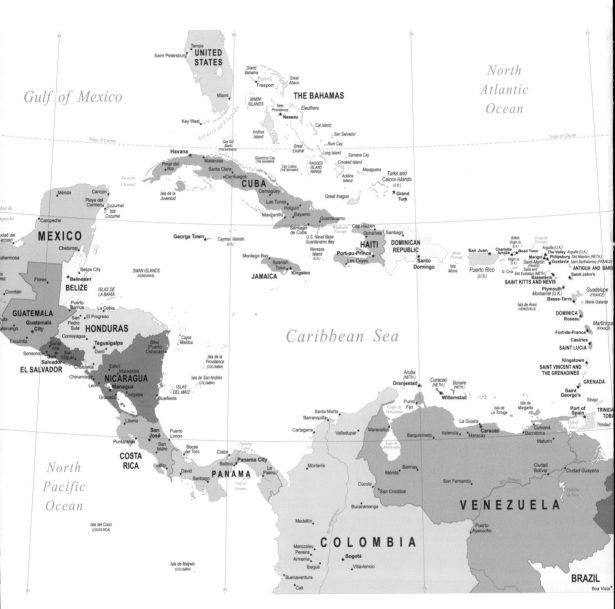

This political map shows the countries of the region discussed in this book.

Social Progress in Central America and the Caribbean

The tropical countries of Central America and the Caribbean are probably best known as world-class tourist destinations for their white beaches, wide biodiversity, colorful cultures, Maya ruins, and friendly people.

Besides being top vacation spots, these countries share the scars of colonization, slavery, and corrupt leadership. Today most Central American and Caribbean countries have high rates of poverty. Between 30 and 50 percent of the people living in Belize, El Salvador, Nicaragua, and the Dominican Republic and more than half the people in Haiti, Guatemala, and Honduras live in poverty. In some cases international aid and money sent home from family members working in other countries are the only way governments can make progress and families can survive. With such high poverty rates and few jobs, many join criminal organizations that move illegal drugs through Central America and the Caribbean. Ruthless street gangs have also attracted unemployed young men and are inflicting brutal violence across both regions.

This volume explores the level of social progress in the seven countries of Central America (Belize, Guatemala, Honduras, El Salvador, Nicaragua, Costa Rica, and Panama) and the five most populated countries of the Caribbean (Cuba, Jamaica, Haiti, Dominican Republic, and Trinidad and

Tobago). *Social progress* is a society's ability to meet the basic human needs of its citizens, create the building blocks that individuals and communities use to improve the quality of their lives, and make it possible for everyone to reach their potential.

To understand how social progress differs from one country to another, the Social Progress Imperative scored 133 countries around the world in three categories:

Basic Human Needs: *Do all people have food, water, shelter, and access to basic medical care? Are they safe?*

Foundations of Well-being: *Do all people get a basic education? Does everyone have health care? Is the environment sustainable?*

Opportunity: *Do people have personal rights and freedoms? Can they participate in the political process?*

Based on dozens of scores in these three areas, the Social Progress Imperative calculated an overall Social Progress Index (SPI) score for each country. Scores were then classified into six groups, from very low social progress to very high. (Belize, Haiti, and Trinidad and Tobago had enough data for only some of the SPI categories, so their overall scores could not be calculated.) As shown in the following table, three of the nine ranked countries fell into the high or upper middle ranks; the rest fell into the lower middle rank. Actual scores for each country can be found in Chapter 4.

Countries around the world are using SPI scores and rankings to identify areas for improvement and to help guide social investment. Even cities will soon be able to evaluate and compare their levels of social progress as the

Income	Country	Social Progress
High	Trinidad and Tobago (C)	*
Upper middle	Panama (CA)	Upper middle
	Costa Rica (CA)	High
	Dominican Republic (C)	Lower middle
	Jamaica (C)	Upper middle
	Belize (CA)	*
Lower middle	El Salvador (CA)	Lower middle
	Guatemala (CA)	Lower middle
	Cuba** (C)	Lower middle
	Nicaragua (CA)	Lower middle
	Honduras (CA)	Lower middle
Low	Haiti (C)	*

C, Caribbean; CA, Central America.

* No overall rank because of incomplete data.

** Rank for Cuba based on 2013 data. All others are from 2014.

Social Progress Imperative releases more city-level scores like those recently published for 10 cities in Colombia (socialprogressimperative.org/data/spi/countries/COL).

The chapters that follow explore some of the stories behind the scores and look at some of the reasons for countries' strengths and weaknesses. You'll see how wealth and social progress are not always related and how a good score does not necessarily mean that improved social progress applies to everyone.

A Nicaraguan woman cooks food in a popular neighborhood of Managua, where food shortages can be a problem.

CHAPTER 1

BASIC HUMAN NEEDS

Words to Understand

Communicable diseases: diseases transmitted from one person or animal to another. Also called contagious or infectious diseases. Example diseases include measles, influenza, malaria, hepatitis, and rabies.

Gross domestic product (GDP): the total value of all products and services created in a country during a year.

GDP per capita (per person): the gross domestic product divided by the number of people in the country. For example, if the GDP for a country is one hundred million dollars ($100,000,000) and the population is one million people (1,000,000), then the GDP per capita (value created per person) is $100.

Income inequality: when the wealth of a country is spread unevenly among the population and the income gap between the rich and the poor is very large.

Undernourishment: not getting enough food or good-quality food to promote health or proper growth.

Meeting basic human needs is the first step toward social progress. Basic needs are the things that people need to live: enough food, clean water, improved sanitation, adequate shelter, and access to basic medical care. People also need to be safe and to feel safe. In 1948 the organization that has become today's Organization of American States (OAS) adopted the American Declaration of the Rights and Duties of Man. Article IX defines the right of people to have their basic needs met:

Every person has the right to the preservation of his health through sanitary and social measures relating to food, clothing, housing and medical care, to the extent permitted by public and community resources.

As members of the OAS, the seven Central American countries and five Caribbean island nations covered in this volume have agreed to work toward this goal. To see how well these and other countries are providing for the most basic of human needs, the Social Progress Imperative looked at 133 countries around the world and ranked them on the Social Progress Index (SPI) in four categories:

Water and Sanitation: *Can people drink the water without getting sick?*
Nutrition and Basic Medical Care: *Do people have enough to eat? Can they see a doctor?*
Shelter: *Do people have housing with basic utilities, such as electricity?*
Personal Safety: *Are people safe from violence? Do they feel afraid?*

The following table shows the countries with the highest and lowest overall scores and their rankings among the 133 SPI countries.

The red and blue numbers in the table show how the size of a country's economy is not the only thing that determines social progress. Sometimes countries score higher (relative strength) or lower (relative weakness) than expected when compared to other countries around the world with similar economics, considered in terms of **GDP** and **GDP per capita**. Costa Rica, for

	Central America		Caribbean	
	Costa Rica **#1 (of 6)**	**El Salvador** **#6 (of 6)**	**Cuba** **#1 (of 5)**	**Haiti** **#5 (of 5)**
	Score (Rank)	Score (Rank)	Score (Rank)	Score (Rank)
GDP per capita	$13,431	$7,515	n/a	$1,648
Nutrition/Medical	96.60 (59th)	90.28 (81st)	97.71 (46th)	47.60 (u)
Water/Sanitation	92.65 (48th)	74.19 (83rd)	85.20 (61st)	25.93 (u)
Shelter	81.98 (30th)	73.94 (48th)	63.14 (81st)	22.58 (u)
Personal Safety	65.65 (63rd)	35.12 (123rd)	74.29 (38th)	47.98 (u)
Overall Basic Human Needs	84.22 (41st)	68.38 (80th)	80.08 (56th)	36.02 (u)

Source: Social Progress Index (SPI).

n/a, not available; u, unranked.

Note: Rankings are among the 133 SPI countries. Some countries could not be ranked because of missing data. No Overall Basic Human Needs score could be calculated for Belize (Central America), so the regional comparison is for six countries instead of seven.

* The GDP ranking shown is the rank among the 133 SPI countries.

example, is one of the richest countries in Central America and has the top overall score for that region. The blue color shows that the score is also higher than the scores of countries with economies of the same size as Costa Rica's, such as Brazil, Dominican Republic, China, and South Africa. Costa Rica's score in the Shelter category is also higher than would be expected if money were the only thing needed to achieve social progress.

Income inequality is often the main cause of low scores for rich countries. Oxfam (oxfam.org), a charity that fights poverty, estimates that by 2016 the richest 1 percent of the world's population will have more wealth than the other 99 percent combined.

At the other end of the scale, red scores highlight countries that are relatively weak when compared to countries with similar economies. El Salvador, for example, has a similar GDP per capita as countries like Bolivia in South America (rank 70th) and Morocco in Africa (rank 49th), but it ranks much lower (123rd) in Personal Safety. Haiti's score in the Nutrition and Basic Medical Care category was even lower than expected for a low-income country. In the sections that follow, we'll look deeper into the reasons behind these scores.

Nutrition and Basic Medical Care

Imagine that your family doesn't get enough to eat. Open sewers and uncovered water tanks in your neighborhood attract flies and breed mosquitoes that spread disease. Many people in your community are sick but can't afford a doctor. Children often die before their fifth birthday. This is reality for the millions of people in the world who live without proper nutrition and clean water and the 2.4 billion people without improved sanitation facilities.

People are undernourished when they don't get enough food or when they don't get enough of the foods that provide the right balance of complete protein, vitamins, and minerals to grow and maintain an active body. Undernourishment causes poor physical condition, health problems, and learning disabilities.

Widespread undernourishment has many causes, including natural disasters; political, social, or economic instability; high food prices; poverty;

Spotlight on Haiti

Haiti survived brutal slavery under the French colonists to become the first independent nation of Latin America and the Caribbean in 1804 following a slave revolt. It has experienced violent border conflicts, a foreign takeover, ruthless dictators, environmental devastation, and deadly natural disasters. When a powerful earthquake hit its crowded capital city, Port-au-Prince, in 2010, Haiti was already a desperately poor country with no way to feed itself.

Before the earthquake, 500,000 Haitians lived in this slum built on a garbage dump.

The earthquake killed 230,000 people and displaced two million. The country survived, but recovery has been slow. Haiti still depends on international aid for much of its food, medical care, and repair of infrastructure, such as buildings, roads, and utilities.

Haiti is the poorest country in the Americas (North, Central, and South America). More than three of every four Haitians live on less than $2 a day. It's not surprising, then, that Haiti scores much lower than any of the other countries in the Caribbean or Central America in the categories of Nutrition and Basic Medical Care, Water and Sanitation, and Shelter.

Haitians evacuate by ship after a powerful earthquake left millions homeless, injured, and hungry.

More than half of the country's 10 million people are undernourished. On average, people in Haiti need an additional 523 calories each day to be properly fed, which is more than half the number of calories needed each day for a two-year-old or 20 percent of an adult's needs. In some areas, women make "cookies" from dried mud mixed with a little flour, sugar, and oil, when they are available. The cookies sell for 5 cents each, and mothers buy them so their children will have something in their stomachs to stop the feeling of hunger for a while.

Fewer than half of the people in rural parts of Haiti have access to a water source that's protected from contamination. Only about 1 in 4 people have access to improved sanitation facilities, and fewer than 10 of every 100 people have access to piped water. More than six years after the earthquake, tens of thousands of Haitians still wait for permanent housing in tent camps.

A corn farmer in Guatemala. Guatemala has been experiencing several years of drought, which has left nearly a million people struggling to feed themselves.

unemployment; trade imbalances; and dependence on imports. People without money for healthy foods buy cheaper, less nutritious foods instead.

In Central America drought has disrupted corn production and left many without enough food to eat. In five of the seven countries, more than 10 percent of the population is undernourished. In Belize 6.5 percent are undernourished, and in Costa Rica, 5.9 percent.

According to the World Bank, unequal access to health care is the number one killer of mothers and children. Most doctors, clinics, and hospitals are located in cities. People who live in rural areas (outside cities) are often poor and can't afford to travel for treatment. They die from communicable diseases caused by bacteria, viruses, and parasites that could have been prevented or cured with basic medical care.

Haiti is the only low-income country in the Caribbean and Central America. It's not surprising, then, that it has the highest number of people that die each year from communicable diseases in either region, 13 times as many as in Costa Rica and 12 times as many as in Cuba. Trinidad and Tobago, the only high-income country in either region, had more deaths from communicable diseases than other countries around the world with similar wealth.

Undernourishment and lack of access to medical care can cause mothers to die during childbirth and children to die before they are 5 years old. The Caribbean, the Dominican Republic, and Trinidad and Tobago had higher deaths in both of these categories than other countries with similar economies. In Central America, Honduras and Nicaragua had fewer child deaths than similar lower-middle-income countries.

Water and Sanitation

Contaminated water and poor sanitation spread diseases like diarrhea, cholera, typhoid, hepatitis, dengue fever, polio, and malaria. These diseases can be a death sentence for people who don't have access to vaccines and basic medical care. The following table shows the two highest and two lowest scores in each region in the categories that the Social Progress Imperative used to calculate overall Water and Sanitation scores.

	CENTRAL AMERICA				CARIBBEAN			
	Costa Rica	Belize	El Salvador	Nicaragua	Trinidad and Tobago	Cuba	Dominican Republic	Haiti
% Rural improved water	90.90	100.00	81.00	67.80	93.10	87.30	77.20	47.50
% Improved sanitation	93.90	90.50	70.50	52.10	92.10	92.60	82.00	24.40
% Access to piped water	95.90	79.10	73.10	63.50	75.80	76.70	66.50	8.70
Overall water/sanitation	92.65	91.17	74.19	59.53	87.51	85.20	74.32	25.93

Haiti is the poorest country and has the lowest scores in either region, but it scores about the same as for other poor countries in the world. Trinidad and Tobago is the richest country in either region, but the red color shows that its scores are lower than expected for a high-income country. Nicaragua has the lowest score in Central America, but the blue color indicates that it is relatively strong compared to other countries around the world with similar economies. Costa Rica's access to piped water is the best in either region, and it is also better than other countries with similar economies, such as the Dominican Republic, which is relatively weak in every category.

Shelter

People need adequate shelter with reliable utilities to keep them safe and healthy. Of the 133 SPI countries, Costa Rica ranked 30th in the Shelter category, scoring higher than every other country in Central America and the Caribbean and also better than other countries around the world with similar economies.

Ninety-nine percent of Costa Ricans have access to electricity compared to about 74 percent in Nicaragua and only about 34 percent in Haiti. Costa Rica also has a low number of deaths that are caused by indoor air pollution from activities such as burning candles and cooking on open fires, reliable electricity, and the third highest level of satisfaction (48 percent) with the affordability of housing in Central America.

Nicaragua scored much lower than Costa Rica but better than other countries in its economic class. The Dominican Republic ranked much lower (83rd) than Costa Rica (30th) even though its economy is a similar size. Haiti's score was weak in the Shelter category, even compared to scores of other poor countries.

The Dominican Republic, Honduras, Guatemala, and Panama were the only countries in the Caribbean and Central America where more than half the people surveyed said they were satisfied with the availability of affordable housing in their area. With 60 percent, El Salvador had the most satisfied people. Only 43 percent were satisfied with the housing situation in Honduras, where, according to Habitat for Humanity (habitat.org), 750,000 of the houses in Honduras need improvements, and over 400,000 families need new homes. (Habitat for Humanity is a nonprofit organization that raises money and finds volunteers to build houses for poor families around the world.)

Personal Safety

Many countries in Central America and the Caribbean have high murder rates, high levels of violent crime, and low levels of trust between citizens. Much of the violence is related to competing criminal organizations fighting to control the highly profitable smuggling of illegal drugs and undocumented migrants into

El Salvador: Guns, Drugs, and Not Enough to Eat

El Salvador is the smallest and most densely populated country in Central America. Extreme poverty, civil war, and natural disasters have shaped Salvadoran society. Thirty-six of every 100 people in El Salvador live below the national poverty line, and more than half of the children under 5 years old are undernourished.

Today, the country is dealing with uncontrolled crime from violent gangs. The gangs profit from drugs, kidnapping, and murder and use extortion to take things or money from people using force or threats. Gangs have even taken homes by telling the owners to leave or be attacked.

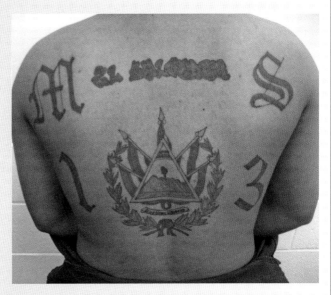

MS 13 (MS XIII) gang tattoo. MS 13 and the 18th Street gangs are two of the largest rival gangs in El Salvador. Both originated in Los Angeles, California, in the 1980s and are known for their cruelty and extreme violence.

There are about 50,000 gang members between the ages of 12 and 55 in El Salvador. Including family members, about 1 of every 10 Salvadorans depends on gangs. A 2012 truce between rival gangs ended in 2015. The violence that followed was extreme. By September of that year, more than 3,800 people had been murdered, 907 in August alone. Gangs killed rival gangs and their families and the police. It was reported that police and military death squads were responsible for many of the killings. This increase in violence put El Salvador on its way to replacing Honduras as the murder capital of the world.

the United States. Gangs that deal in narcotics and guns, murder for hire, carjacking, extortion, and violent street crime also make life dangerous in many countries.

Trinidad and Tobago had the lowest Personal Safety score of any high-income country in the world. El Salvador (123rd), Guatemala (119th), Honduras (127th), the Dominican Republic (125th), and Jamaica (118th) all rank in the bottom 25 percent of the 133 SPI countries in Personal Safety. These countries plus Panama all had some of the highest murder rates anywhere, and all scored lower than countries with similar economies.

Violent crime is high in El Salvador, Guatemala, Honduras, Jamaica, and Trinidad and Tobago. There is also high distrust between citizens in these countries. None of the countries in these regions scored as well as their economic equals.

The highest scores in Personal Safety in Central America were Costa Rica, Nicaragua, and Panama; all scored about the same as countries with similar economies. In the Caribbean, Cuba had the highest Personal Safety score (74.29, rank 38th), which was more than twice as high as the score of the Dominican Republic (34.95, rank 125th). Jamaica scored higher than expected for its economy; Trinidad and Tobago scored worse than other wealthy countries. Haiti is the only country in either region where the murder rate is a relative strength compared to countries with similar economies.

Traffic accidents are another safety issue. The best place in Central America to avoid a deadly traffic accident is Guatemala, which ranks 18th in the number of traffic deaths of the 133 SPI countries. El Salvador ranks a dangerous 101st. In the Caribbean, people in the Dominican Republic had the highest number of traffic deaths of all the SPI countries. People there are five times more likely to die in a traffic accident than those in Cuba.

Helmet laws are often not enforced in the Dominican Republic, which contributes to the high number of traffic deaths in that country.

Text-Dependent Questions

1. What are three causes of widespread undernourishment?
2. A higher GDP does not always mean higher social progress. Why?
3. Which country in Central America has the highest overall Social Progress score? In the Caribbean?
4. Why is El Salvador becoming the murder capital of the world?
5. Rich countries usually score higher in social progress than poor countries. How do relative strengths (blue scores) and relative weaknesses (red scores) help us understand how well countries are providing basic human needs for their citizens?

Research Project

Explore the results of the 2000–2015 Millennium Development Goals (MDGs) and the new targets for the 2015–2030 Sustainable Development Goals (SDGs).

1. In 2000 the United Nations (UN) named eight goals for ending poverty in the world by 2015. Four of the goals were about meeting basic human needs. Go to the MDG web page on the United Nations website: http://www.un.org/millenniumgoals/. On the web page, click each of the icons shown below to learn what was accomplished for each and answer the questions that follow:

Were extreme poverty rates cut in half? By how much did child mortality drop from 1990 to 2015? Were maternal deaths reduced by the desired amount of three-fourths? What was accomplished toward combating HIV/AIDS, malaria, and other diseases?

2. Go to the UN's web page for the Sustainable Development Goals (2015–2030): https://sustainabledevelopment.un.org/topics

   On the web page, expand the goals shown below and select the *Goal Targets* tab to learn what's planned for each of these goals. Then, use the information you find about each goal to fill in the blanks in the sentences that follow.

Goal 1: No Poverty. *By 2030 eradicate extreme poverty for all people everywhere, currently measured as people living on less than $_____ a day.*

Goal 2: Zero Hunger. *By 2030 end hunger and ensure access by _____, in particular the poor and people in vulnerable situations, including infants, to _____, _____, _____, and _____ food year-round.*

Goal 3: Good Health. *By 2030 reduce the global _____ _____ ratio to less than 70 per 100,000 live births [and] . . . end preventable deaths of newborns and children under _____ years of age.*

Goal 6: Clean Water and Sanitation. *By 2030 improve water quality by _____ _____, _____ _____, and minimizing release of _____ _____ and materials, halving the proportion of untreated wastewater and substantially increasing recycling and safe reuse globally.*

Schoolgirls make their way in the central highlands of Costa Rica.

CHAPTER 2

FOUNDATIONS OF WELL-BEING

Words to Understand

Adult literacy rate: the percentage of adults (age 15 and older) who can read and write.

Life expectancy: the average amount of time a person is expected to live at birth.

Nongovernmental organization (NGO): a nonprofit, voluntary citizens' group organized on a local, national, or international level. Examples include organizations that support human rights, advocate for political participation, and work for improved health care.

Primary education: generally, basic education for children (usually ages 5 to 11), including reading, writing, and basic math. For most countries, primary education is mandatory. Also called elementary education.

Secondary education: includes two levels, lower and upper. Lower secondary education follows the primary level and is usually mandatory. After completing the lower secondary level, many students enter the workforce while others continue their schooling. Upper secondary education is the final level of secondary education. Entrance to this level is usually at 15 or 16 years old.

Real social progress goes further than simply having the basics to stay alive. People also need to be educated and allowed to develop the skills that will help them improve the quality of their lives. They need an environment that gives them a sense of well-being, an environment that makes them feel comfortable, healthy, and happy.

To compare how well countries around the world provide the building blocks that citizens and communities use to create better lives, the Social Progress Imperative looked at 133 countries in four areas:

Access to Basic Knowledge: *Can children go to school? Can adults read and write?*

Access to Information and Communications: *Do people have Internet access? Cell phones? Is the news they hear and read controlled by the government or special interests?*

Health and Wellness: *How long do people live? Do they die early from treatable diseases?*

Ecosystem Sustainability: *Will future generations live in a healthy environment?*

The following table shows the countries with the highest and lowest overall scores and rankings in these Foundations of Well-being for the seven countries of Central America and the five most populated Caribbean island nations.

Costa Rica's political stability, high standard of living, and well-developed social benefits system set it apart from other countries in Central America and the Caribbean. It has the top score in either region in the Foundations of Well-being and shows relative strengths (blue scores) overall and in Health and Wellness and Access to Information and Communications when compared to countries with economies of the same size. Belize, the lowest-scoring Central American country in Foundations of Well-being, also shows a relative weakness (red scores) in its overall score and in the Access to Information and Communications and Ecosystem Sustainability categories.

	Central America		Caribbean	
	Costa Rica **#1 (of 7)** GDP PC: $13,431	**Belize** **#6 (of 7)** GDP PC: $8,215	**Jamaica** **#1 (of 3)** GDP PC: $8,607	**Cuba** **#3 (of 3)** GDP PC: n/a
	Score (Rank)	Score (Rank)	Score (Rank)	Score (Rank)
Access Basic Knowledge	93.96 (56th)	89.98 (u)	90.64 (74th)	96.03 (39th)
Health and Wellness	78.09 (8th)	71.50 (u)	93.45 (35th)	73.29 (36th)
Access to Information and Communications	80.66 (35th)	59.03 (u)	78.98 (93rd)	24.33 (132nd)
Ecosystem Sustainability	62.61 (63rd)	41.73 (u)	48.28 (40th)	48.38 (92nd)
Overall Foundations of Well-being	78.83 (17th)	65.56 (u)	72.84 (49th)	60.51 (105th)

Source: Social Progress Index (SPI).

n/a = not available; u = unranked.

Note: Rankings are among the 133 SPI countries. Some countries could not be ranked because of incomplete data. No Overall Foundations of Well-being score could be calculated for Haiti or Trinidad and Tobago, so the regional comparison is for three countries instead of five. GDP PC stands for gross domestic product per capita (per person). GDP is equal to the total value of all products and services created in a country during a year. GDP PC is the gross domestic product divided by the number of people in the country. Cuba is not included in the comparisons to countries with similar economies.

Of the five Caribbean countries, complete scores were available only for Cuba, the Dominican Republic, and Jamaica. Of those three, Jamaica scored the highest and also showed a relative strength in Access to Information and Communications. Cuba had the lowest overall score in spite of having the highest score in either region in Access to Basic Knowledge. Low scores in Ecosystem Sustainability and in Access to Information and Communications brought down its average score. Both Haiti and Trinidad and Tobago had lower scores than Cuba in several areas, but incomplete data made it impossible to calculate scores in the main categories that make up the overall Foundations of Well-being score. In the sections that follow, we'll look deeper into the reasons behind these scores.

Access to Basic Knowledge

A basic education is necessary to achieve social progress in any country. Education and poverty are linked. Children of uneducated parents learn less at home and have fewer opportunities to go to school, which creates a cycle of poverty that continues from one generation to the next.

In some countries, girls have fewer opportunities to go to school than boys do. Fortunately, girls have an equal opportunity to go to school through

Girls participate equally with boys in schools in El Salvador, where more than 93 percent of the children who should be in primary school are enrolled.

the upper secondary (high school) level in every Central American and Caribbean country except Guatemala. Guatemala ranked 99th among the SPI countries and showed a relative weakness compared to its economic equals. (No scores were available for Haiti or Trinidad and Tobago in this category.)

The highest adult literacy rate in Central America is in Costa Rica, where almost 98 percent of adults can read and write. Haiti, where only about 60 percent of the people are literate, had the lowest score in the Caribbean. In Central America, Guatemala scored lowest, with only about 82 percent of adults able to read and write. Adult literacy was a relative weakness for Guatemala compared to the percentage of literate adults in countries with similar economies.

Cuba: Everyone Reads!

At 99.85 percent, Cuba has one of the highest adult literacy rates in the world. More people in Cuba can read than in any other country in the Caribbean or Central America, more than in the United States or in Canada.

Universal literacy was not always the case in Cuba. Before the Cuban Revolution (1953–1959), only about half of Cuba's children went to school, and more than 40 percent of the rural population was illiterate. After the Cuban Revolution ended, one of the first goals of the new socialist government was to put an end to illiteracy. In 1961, more than 250,000 Cubans joined their country's National Literacy Campaign and spread across the country to teach more than 700,000 illiterate Cubans to read and write. Nearly half of the volunteer teachers were under 18 and more than half were women. By 1969, the literacy rate in Cuba was close to 100 percent.

Cuba maintains its high literacy rate by supporting free mandatory **primary** and lower **secondary education** for all children. Children must attend school from age 6 to 15 or 16. Less than 1.0 percent of students drop out of primary school, and 98.2 percent continue their studies after the sixth grade. Cuba has the highest primary and lower secondary enrollments in either the Caribbean or Central America and the second highest upper secondary enrollments in either region after Jamaica. More than 90 percent of high-school-aged youth in Jamaica are in school. It ranked 44th of the SPI countries, which is higher than the United States (49th) and very impressive for a country with only the 78th largest economy of the countries ranked by the SPI.

The Dominican Republic ranked in the bottom one-third of the 133 SPI countries in primary and lower secondary enrollments, and both categories were relative weaknesses. Even though Trinidad and Tobago has much higher enrollments than the Dominican Republic, they were lower than expected for a high-income country.

Health and Wellness

Every country has its own system of health care. All the systems have the same goal, which is to provide health care for everyone and protect people from financial ruin from high medical bills. Some countries have universal health care, where everyone has health insurance under the same system. These systems are run by the government and paid for by the public with taxes.

Costa Rica and Cuba provide universal health care for their citizens. If you are Costa Rican, you can expect, on average, to live 79.7 years, which is six months longer than a Cuban, one year longer than an American, and almost 18 years

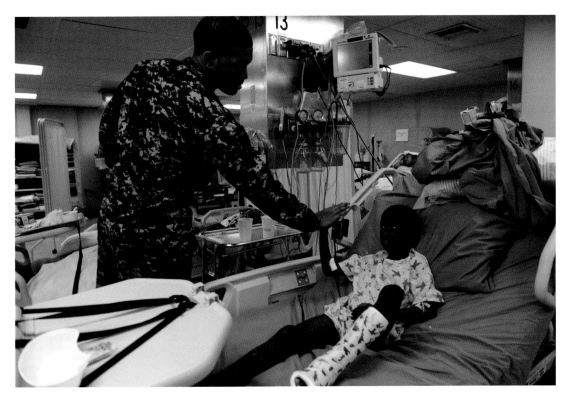

A Jamaican boy receives physical therapy on board a United States military hospital ship during its five-month humanitarian assistance mission to the Caribbean, Central America, and South America.

longer than a Haitian. Life expectancy is a relative strength for Honduras and Nicaragua; it's a relative weakness in Trinidad and Tobago.

Unfortunately, even when everyone has insurance, not everyone has equal access to doctors and hospitals. Overall access to health care is lower in countries with high poverty rates or large rural populations. Even in countries with universal care, private health insurance is available to those who can pay for it. Private insurance can mean access to the best doctors, specialists, and hospitals.

Access to Information and Communications

Cell phones and Internet access have become important tools for getting and sharing information. People need information they can trust so that they can make good decisions and stay safe. The SPI scores in this category show the level of freedom that citizens have to access information and ideas in their countries.

Internet and cell phone use

Despite having the lowest score in the Caribbean in Health and Wellness, Trinidad and Tobago is at the top of the list in Access to Information and

A man uses his desktop computer in an apartment in Havana, Cuba. In 2016 the state telecommunications company announced the launch of the broadband home Internet service through Chinese telecom operator Huawei.

Communications with high numbers of Internet users (64 percent) and cell phone subscriptions (more than one per person). Even so, Internet use in Trinidad and Tobago is lower than expected for a high-income country. Only about 11 percent of the people use the Internet in Haiti, 26 percent in Cuba.

Cuba had the lowest Internet access in the Western Hemisphere (includes North, Central, and South America and the Caribbean) and ranked 132nd of the 133 SPI countries in Access to Information and Communications. To use the Internet in Cuba, people must go to access points controlled by the government where many websites are blocked, browser histories are checked, and keywords are filtered. Cuba was rated "not free" in 2011–2014 in an annual study of Internet freedom around the world produced by Freedom House (freedomhouse.org), a nongovernmental organization (NGO) that conducts research and promotes democracy, political freedom, and human rights.

In Central America, Costa Rica had the highest Internet use at 46 percent; Nicaragua had the lowest at only about 16 percent. Panama, Guatemala, and El Salvador all had more than one cell phone subscription per person, but in Belize fewer than half the people had mobile phones.

Press freedom index

As part of the Access to Information and Communications score, the Social Progress Imperative used the Press Freedom Index. (In journalism, the press are the news media companies and the people who work for them.) The index is created each year by Reporters Without Borders (rsf.org), an NGO that promotes freedom of information and freedom of the press. Index scores are based on four main categories:

Fairness of the news media (print, broadcast, and online): *Are both sides of a story told? Are all cultural and political groups treated fairly in the news?*

Independence of news media: *Are most of the news outlets owned by the government or by just a few companies that control what people read and hear?*

Level of respect for the safety/freedom of journalists: *Do reporters face violence or jail for doing their jobs?*

Working environment for the news media: *Do the laws protect journalists? Are the media afraid of the government? Organized crime? Terrorists?*

In 2014 Reporters Without Borders classified the freedom of the press in Central America and the five SPI Caribbean countries as follows:

Good Situation →	Costa Rica, Jamaica
Satisfactory Situation→	Belize, El Salvador, Trinidad and Tobago
Noticeable Problems→	Guatemala, Honduras, Nicaragua, Dominican Republic, Haiti
Difficult Situation→	No countries
Very Serious Situation→	Cuba

Cuba was included in the 2015 list of the 10 Most Censored Countries published by the Committee to Protect Journalists (cpj.org). The government, for example, has put journalists in prison for sending reports out of the country through the Internet.

Ecosystem Sustainability

If an activity is not sustainable, there will come a time when it's no longer possible to do it. For example, if you take money from your savings account every month without putting any money into it, that activity is not sustainable because at some point the account will run out of money. Ecosystem sustainability is when we care for natural resources like clean air, water, plants, and animals in such a way that they will still be here for future generations. To measure ecosystem sustainability, the Social Progress Imperative compared countries in three categories: greenhouse gas emissions, water use, and protection of habitat and species. Unfortunately, companies doing business in countries that are rich in natural resources but poor in regulation can earn large profits at the expense of the environment.

Panama (68.88), Honduras (67.91), and Nicaragua (67.40) had the top scores in Ecosystem Sustainability in Central America. All ranked in the top 20 of the 133 SPI countries. In the Caribbean, the Dominican Republic (56.42) earned the top score. The lowest-ranking countries were El Salvador (95th), Jamaica (93rd), and Cuba (92nd).

Costa Rica has been recognized for its efforts to protect the environment. It has been listed as the greenest country in the world by the New Economics Foundation (NEF, neweconomics.org) and was the highest ranking country on the NEF's 2012 Happy Planet Index, which considers such things as ecological footprint, or the effects of human activities on the environment. In 2012 it became the first country in the region to ban recreational hunting.

Biodiversity and habitat

Biodiversity is the variety of plant and animal life in an area. Habitat is the environment in which a plant or animal needs to live. Cutting down forests for agriculture, wood, and space for development destroys habitats and reduces biodiversity by causing some plants and animals to become extinct. Water pollution, air pollution, and the effects of climate change also destroy habitats that plants and animals need to live. Human activities such as deforestation, hunting, fishing, collecting animals for the pet trade, and introducing nonnative animals also reduce biodiversity.

The ocellated turkey is hunted for food and sport in Belize, which, along with deforestation, has put it on the list of endangered species.

With only 0.01 percent of the world's land area, Central America has 7 percent of the world's biodiversity. Panama and Costa Rica are the most diverse countries, followed by Guatemala and Belize. Belize (unranked) and Nicaragua (ranked 22nd) had the highest SPI scores in the region for protecting biodiversity and habitats; it was a relative strength for both countries. El Salvador had the lowest score in Central America and ranked a very low 115th of the 133 SPI countries.

The last golden toad was seen in Costa Rica in 1989. Drought, pollution, pesticides, and climate change are thought to have caused its extinction.

Cuba has the most biodiversity in the Caribbean but ranks 83rd in protection. The Dominican Republic had the highest score and ranked an impressive 17th of the 133 SPI countries. Haiti was by far the lowest scoring of all the countries in either region. Originally a plantation colony, most of the forests in Haiti were cleared for agriculture long ago. Today, only 2 percent of Haiti's forests remain.

The Cuban crocodile has been hunted almost to extinction.
It is listed as critically endangered.

Greenhouse gas emissions

Gases that trap heat in the earth's atmosphere are called greenhouse gases. Some of these gases are found naturally in the environment; others are released by the activities of humans. Carbon dioxide is the most common greenhouse gas. It's released when people burn coal, natural gas, or oil. Plants absorb carbon dioxide, so when forests are cut or land is cleared for houses, even more carbon dioxide gets into the atmosphere.

Measuring greenhouse gas emissions is important because they have been linked to global warming and climate change. Global warming is expected to have a negative effect on the environment by increasing the average world temperature, which will change where and how much it rains and snows, reduce ice and snow cover, raise the sea level, and increase ocean acidity.

Costa Rica and Panama had the lowest greenhouse gas emissions in Central America; Nicaragua and Belize had the highest. In the Caribbean, Cuba had the lowest emissions; Trinidad and Tobago—with its large petroleum and natural gas production—had the highest.

Water stress

Water stress is measured by how much water a country has compared to how much it uses for all purposes, including for agriculture, industry, and personal use. Countries with medium, high, and extremely high water stress levels will need to work quickly to manage their water resources to avoid severe shortages in the near future.

Water Stress	Central America	Caribbean
Low	Honduras, Panama	
Low medium	Belize, El Salvador, Guatemala, Nicaragua	
Medium high	Costa Rica	Haiti
High		Cuba, Dominican Republic
Extremely high		Jamaica, Trinidad and Tobago

Text-Dependent Questions

1. Is water stress higher in Central America or in the Caribbean?
2. True or false: Cuba has a higher literacy rate than Canada.
3. How many more years does the average Costa Rican live than the average Haitian?

Research Project

Visit Earth's Endangered Creatures website at earthsendangered .com. Select Central America from the list of species profiles in the left column. On the Endangered Mammals of Central America page that appears, click the link for red-backed squirrel monkey. Use the information on the page to answer the following: When was the creature listed as endangered? What are the causes of the population decline?

Hundreds attend the funer
Honduran activist Berta Cac
in La Esperanza, Honduras.
prominent environment
advocated for the righ
indigenous people. Unkn
assailants shot her dead in
he

CHAPTER 3

OPPORTUNITY

To reach our potential, we need freedom and opportunity. We want the freedom to move around, practice our religions, and make our own choices. We want an equal opportunity to get a college degree and have a voice in the political process. To better understand how the level of opportunity differs from one country to another, the Social Progress Imperative scored 133 countries in the following categories:

Personal Freedom and Choice: *Are people allowed to make their own decisions?*

Tolerance and Inclusion: *Does everyone have the same opportunity to contribute?*

Access to Advanced Education: *Does everyone have the opportunity to go to college?*

Personal Rights: *Are people's individual rights restricted by the government?*

The table below shows the SPI Opportunity scores and rankings of the seven Central American countries and the five Caribbean countries considered in this volume.

Region	Country	Score	Rank
Central America	Costa Rica	70.59	25th
Caribbean	Jamaica	66.14	31st
Caribbean	Trinidad and Tobago	63.83	u
Central America	Panama	61.90	38th
Central America	El Salvador	55.75	55th
Central America	Nicaragua	48.58	72nd
Central America	Guatemala	48.29	74th
Central America	Honduras	46.32	79th
Caribbean	Dominican Republic	50.65	66th
Caribbean	Cuba	41.90	97th
Caribbean	Haiti	36.89	u
Central America	Belize	n/a	u

n/a, not available; u, unranked.
Rankings are among the 133 SPI countries.

Costa Rica and Jamaica had strong scores in Opportunity, and Trinidad and Tobago and Panama also scored in the top one-third of the SPI countries in Opportunity. Cuba's overall score was low because of low scores in Personal Freedom and Choice and the lowest score in the world in Personal Rights. Haiti has the lowest score in either region but didn't score lower than other very poor countries. In the sections that follow, we'll look deeper into the reasons behind these scores.

Overall scores for the countries are important, but looking at how they compare with countries with similar economies is also interesting and useful. The table below shows the number of categories in which each country scored unexpectedly higher (relative strength) or unexpectedly lower than their economic peers. It also shows into which income class each country falls.

Numbers of Relative Strengths and Weaknesses in Opportunity			
Income	Country	Strengths	Weaknesses
High	Trinidad and Tobago	1	8
Upper middle	Panama	4	4
	Costa Rica	12	3
	Dominican Republic	1	8
	Jamaica	8	0
	Belize	4	1
Lower middle	El Salvador	2	3
	Guatemala	3	8
	Cuba	*	*
	Nicaragua	5	3
	Honduras	3	2
Low	Haiti	2	5

Sources: Income rankings are from the World Bank. Strengths and Weaknesses are from SPI.

* Relative comparisons based on income were not available.

Personal Freedom and Choice

Scores in the category of Personal Freedom and Choice help us understand how much freedom citizens in each country have to make important decisions about things like religion, marriage, and children. It also considers the level of corruption because corruption limits everyone's freedom.

Freedom of religion

Every country in Central America and the Caribbean, except Cuba, scored high in religious freedom. It was a relative strength for El Salvador, Guatemala,

A Hindu festival in Trinidad and Tobago, where more than 18 percent of the people are Hindu. Other religions in the country include Protestant (32.1%), Catholic (2.2%), and Muslim (5%).

Honduras, and Nicaragua. In Cuba the Communist Party has controlled the government since 1965. Official atheism was removed from the constitution in 1992, but churches are still not allowed to provide standard education, and their publications can be censored by the government. The government has granted few permits to build churches over the past 50 years, and worship held in private homes can result in the government taking the property.

Early marriage

Teen marriage makes it hard for young people to take advantage of whatever opportunities are available to them. Marriage before finishing high school usually means leaving school to work. Early marriage for girls 15 to 18 years old often follows pregnancy. Child care can be expensive, so young mothers sometimes have to quit school to stay home with children.

The percentage of women married between the ages of 15 and 19 was a relative weakness for six of the seven Central American countries. (No information was available for Belize.) In some countries, child marriage is also a problem. In Nicaragua, for example, 1 out of every 10 girls is married before age 15, and another 40 percent marry by age 19. This means that half of the females in the country are married by age 19.

In the Caribbean, the Dominican Republic had the highest percentage of early marriages, with 27 percent of young women marrying between 15 and 19 years old. Jamaica (1 percent) and Trinidad and Tobago (3 percent) had by far the lowest percentages of teen marriages in either region.

Freedom over life choices

The table below shows the percentage of people in each country that said they were satisfied with the amount of freedom they have to make choices about their lives:

% Satisfied	Countries
90+	Costa Rica
80–89	Panama, Guatemala, Nicaragua, Dominican Republic, Trinidad and Tobago
70–79	El Salvador, Jamaica
60–69	Honduras, Belize
50–59	Haiti
20–29	Cuba

Corruption

Corruption creates an unfair society that favors some people over others. When people in power take advantage of their positions for their own benefit, we say that they are corrupt or that there is corruption in the system. Corruption often takes the form of officials accepting money or favors (bribes) to break the rules. In the worst cases, it means that the government can use public money for personal gain, the police can be paid to ignore crimes or arrest innocent people, and the courts can be influenced to find someone guilty or innocent.

The following table shows SPI corruption scores derived from data from Transparency International on how much corruption people think is happening in their country. The lower the score, the more corruption people believe there is.

Score		Countries*
71–100		--
51–70	↑ MORE CORRUPTION	Costa Rica
41–50	LESS CORRUPTION	Cuba
31–40		El Salvador, Guatemala, Panama, Dominican Republic, Jamaica, Trinidad and Tobago
21–30	↓	Honduras, Nicaragua
0–20		Haiti

*No score available for Belize.

Costa Rica ranked highest of the 133 SPI countries, at 33rd. Honduras (101st) and Nicaragua (107th) rank in the bottom 25 percent. Guatemala and the Dominican Republic tied for 93rd. Corruption was a relative weakness in the Dominican Republic, Haiti, and Trinidad and Tobago.

Tolerance and Inclusion

Scores for Tolerance and Inclusion reflect the prejudice in a society that makes it hard for some groups of people to succeed. Prejudice and stereotypes toward indigenous people, racial minorities, immigrants, women, or the poor can result in unfair treatment that denies these groups equal opportunities for housing, education, and jobs. Overall scores in this category were in line with other countries with similar economies in both Central America and the Caribbean. Costa Rica, Nicaragua, Panama, and Jamaica all showed relative strengths in this category.

Most Guna people live in the San Blas Islands off the coast of Panama. There are also groups that live on the mainland and make their living selling fine handcrafts. Gunas have retained much of their own culture and language in spite of Spanish influence.

Religious tolerance

SPI rankings based on data from the Pew Research Center Social Hostilities Index showed a high tolerance for religion throughout Central America and the Caribbean. It was a relative strength for El Salvador, Guatemala, Honduras, and Nicaragua.

Community safety net

A high percentage of people in both Central America and the Caribbean said they have family or friends they can count on if needed. Cuba (97 percent, ranked 16th) and Costa Rica (93 percent) had the most people with this kind of community support; Honduras (79 percent) and Haiti (64 percent) had the fewest.

Discrimination and violence against minorities

Many indigenous people who were present when the first Europeans arrived died out from the previously unknown diseases brought by the colonizers. Others were murdered or enslaved. Many slaves died from physical abuse. Their numbers were replaced with tens of thousands of slaves brought from Africa. Where there are no indigenous people left, black people occupy the bottom rung of the social ladder. Even in countries where blacks make up the majority of the population, discrimination is sometimes based on the darkness of a person's skin.

Costa Rica and Belize showed the least discrimination and violence against minorities in Central America. Guatemala showed the most, with a low ranking of 98th among the SPI countries.

In the Caribbean, Haiti and the Dominican Republic showed the most discrimination and violence against minorities. Haitians themselves are highly discriminated against in the Dominican Republic. In 2013 a Dominican court decision took away the citizenship of 200,000 Dominicans of Haitian descent born after 1929. In 2015 the Dominican Republic deported thousands of Haitian immigrants and Dominican-born people of Haitian descent to Haiti. The action reminded some of the 1937 massacre of thousands of Haitian migrants ordered by the president of the Dominican Republic.

Maya People in Guatemala

The sophisticated Maya civilization existed in parts of Mexico, Belize, Honduras, and Guatemala for thousands of years before the Spanish conquerors arrived. The Spanish came to what is now Guatemala in 1524. They were met with fierce resistance from the Maya city-states, and it was not until 1697 that the last Maya kingdom fell. After the conquest, the Maya people suffered centuries of abuse and discrimination.

Tikal ruins, Guatemala. The Maya civilization was at its height between AD 300 and 900. When the Spanish arrived a few hundred years later, elaborate ritual centers like Tikal were no longer used and almost completely hidden by the jungle.

Guatemala has the largest surviving population of indigenous people in Central America; Maya people make up more than 40 percent of the country's population. In 1960 the Maya joined other poor citizens in a rebellion against the economic injustice and physical hardships inflicted by the Guatemalan ruling class on the poor. When the brutal war ended in 1996, more than 80 percent of the 200,000 that had died were

Mayans. Today most Mayans in Guatemala still live in extreme poverty and have little say in the government or how they are treated.

In 2015 almost 300 Maya families won a 200-year-long battle for legal rights to the land where they have lived and worked for hundreds of years. Their latest problem was with a logging company that had government support to force people off their land to harvest trees. Although the rights of these families were finally upheld, many more have been displaced, and many others remain vulnerable to this kind of government taking of land.

Tolerance for immigrants

In general, people who come from a foreign country (immigrants) are better tolerated the more similar they are to the majority population of the host country. Immigrants who are of a different race, speak a different language, or practice a different religion face discrimination that makes it difficult for them to find acceptable housing and jobs. Immigrants often come to countries with better economies looking for jobs. If the economy weakens and there aren't enough jobs to go around, locals have less tolerance for immigrants in the workforce.

Seventy-five percent of the people in Costa Rica think that the area in which they live is also a good place for immigrants from other countries to live. Only 42 percent of the people in Honduras think so. All the countries in Central America except Costa Rica and El Salvador showed a relative weakness in this category when compared to other countries with similar economies. In the Caribbean, Jamaica had the highest percentage (70 percent). The Dominican Republic shows the least tolerance for immigrants, lower than countries with similar economies.

Tolerance for homosexuals

Although it is not legal for homosexuals to marry in any Central American or Caribbean country, six countries had relative strengths in this category with higher scores than other countries with similar economies: Costa Rica, El Salvador, Honduras, Nicaragua, Panama, and Haiti. The lowest score in either region was in Jamaica, which ranked 89th of the SPI countries.

Access to Advanced Education

Advanced education generally refers to college, or tertiary education. None of the countries of Central America or the Caribbean showed a relative strength in the Access to Advanced Education category. In those two regions, there are only three globally ranked universities in both regions: two in Costa Rica and one in Cuba.

Panama had the highest average years of education past high school in either region at 0.81 year, less than expected for an upper middle–income country. Education after high school was a relative strength in Costa Rica and Nicaragua. Average years of education past high school was zero in Guatemala, which was lower than for countries with similar economies.

Even in countries with good education systems, not everyone can go to college. The following table shows the highest- and lowest-ranking countries in both regions in two measures of inequality: women's average years in school and inequality in the attainment of education, which measures whether or not everyone has the same opportunity to go to school (lower scores show less inequality).

Guatemala showed a relative weakness in all three categories. Even though Haiti had the lowest number of years in school for women, it was still a relative strength compared to other low-income countries.

	Central America		Caribbean	
	Costa Rica #1 (of 7)	Guatemala #7 (of 7)	Cuba #1 (of 5)	Haiti #5 (of 5)
	GDP PC: $13,431	GDP PC: $7,062	GDP PC: n/a	GDP PC: $1,648
	Score (Rank)	Score (Rank)	Score (Rank)	Score (Rank)
Women's average years	10.8 (62nd)	54 (107th)	12.4 (u)	6.1 (u)
Inequality in attainment	0.16 (61st)	0.36 (102nd)	0.11 (u)	0.40 (u)
Overall Access to Adv. Ed	49.24 (58th)	15.34 (117th)	49.52 (u)	15.27 (u)

Source: Social Progress Index (SPI).

n/a, not available.

u, unranked.

Note: Rankings are among the 133 SPI countries. Unranked countries had incomplete data. GDP PC stands for gross domestic product per capita (per person). GDP is equal to the total value of all products and services created in a country during a year. GDP PC is the gross domestic product divided by the number of people in the country. Cuba is not included in the comparisons to countries with similar economies.

Personal Rights

Having personal rights is a necessary part of having opportunities. Personal rights are protected by law in South America, but the laws are not always enforced. People lose their rights when those who violate them are not held accountable by the police and the courts. Personal Rights were a relative strength in Belize, Costa Rica, and Jamaica, and Belize had the highest score in Central America. Personal Rights were a relative weakness for the Dominican Republic. Cuba had the lowest score of any country in either region and ranked at the very bottom (133rd) of the 133 SPI countries in the Personal Rights category.

People should be able to move around their country and travel to other countries and return. The table below shows the level of government restriction placed on citizens in Central America and the Caribbean on the freedoms of movement, association/assembly, and speech.

Of all the countries in Central America and the Caribbean, only Cuba severely restricts foreign (out of the country) and domestic (within the country) travel for its citizens, which gave it a low rank of 126th in this category. Cuba passed a less restrictive travel law in 2013, but the government still reserves the right to deny foreign travel to any citizen to protect national security or

Level	Type of Restriction	Countries
UNRESTRICTED	Foreign movement	Belize, El Salvador, Guatemala, Honduras, Nicaragua, Panama, Haiti, Jamaica, Trinidad and Tobago
	Domestic movement	Belize, Costa Rica, El Salvador, Guatemala, Panama, Haiti, Jamaica, Trinidad and Tobago
	Assembly/association	Belize, Costa Rica, El Salvador, Guatemala, Panama, Jamaica, Trinidad and Tobago
	Speech	Belize, Costa Rica, Jamaica
SOMEWHAT	Foreign movement	Costa Rica, Dominican Republic
	Domestic movement	Dominican Republic, Honduras, Nicaragua
	Assembly/association	Honduras, Nicaragua, Haiti
	Speech	El Salvador, Guatemala, Honduras, Nicaragua, Panama, Dominican Republic, Haiti, Trinidad and Tobago
SEVERE	Foreign movement	Cuba
	Domestic movement	Cuba
	Assembly/association	Cuba, Dominican Republic
	Speech	Cuba

for reasons of the public interest. Within the country, Cubans must obtain government permission before moving to the capital city of Havana. Some have been detained or temporarily jailed on their way to or from church or meetings to talk about politics.

Score		Country
1	↑ FEWER POLITICAL RIGHTS MORE POLITICAL RIGHTS ↓	Belize, Costa Rica,
2		El Salvador, Panama, Dominican Republic, Jamaica, Trinidad and Tobago
3		Guatemala
4		Honduras, Nicaragua
5		Haiti
6		none
7		Cuba

Political rights

For those who enjoy the rights of citizenship and participation in the political process, it can be hard to imagine that citizens of some countries aren't allowed to vote or hold public office, have no say in what their government does, and have no right to complain. SPI scores for political rights, based on data from Freedom House, are shown in the table above.

Private property rights

Opportunity is limited if individuals, corporations, or the government can take personal property from its rightful owner without fear of being taken to court. In many countries, the rural poor, indigenous groups, and people living in poverty have never received legal title to land they've lived on for hundreds of years. These vulnerable populations have little voice in government land distribution decisions and few options after their land is taken for its natural resources or to use for commercial development.

Not a single country in Central America or the Caribbean scored more than 50 points on a 100-point scale measuring private property rights. Guatemala, Nicaragua, Cuba, and Haiti ranked in the bottom 25 percent of the 133 SPI countries. Only Costa Rica (50), Jamaica (40), and Trinidad and Tobago (50) scored in the top 50 percent of the SPI countries.

Text-Dependent Questions

1. Refer to the table on page 49. Which countries were ranked higher in Social Progress than their income level?
2. What percentage of girls and young women are married by age 19 in Nicaragua?
3. In which country is the average number of years of school for women only 5.4 years?
4. In Guatemala what percentage of the population are indigenous Maya people?
5. In which two countries of the Caribbean is freedom of assembly most restricted?

Research Project

Explore the SPI data online to learn more about the relative social progress of Central American and Caribbean countries.

1. Go to the Social Progress Imperative website: socialprogressimperative .org. Click on the Social Progress Index.

2. Click on Display Relative Performance from the list of options on the right of the map. Which Central American and Caribbean countries show relative strengths? Weaknesses?

3. With Relative Performance still selected, click on Opportunity. The map changes to show relative strengths and weakness in the Opportunity category. Click back and forth between Social Progress and Opportunity. Notice how relative strengths and weaknesses change depending on which category is selected.

4. Write a page on what you find, especially noting any surprising relationships.

A child in the band Mix Up leads Carnival revelry during the junior parade in the streets of Port-of-Spain, Trinidad and Tobago.

CHAPTER 4

CENTRAL AMERICAN AND CARIBBEAN COUNTRIES AT A GLANCE

BELIZE

QUICK STATS

Population: 347,369
Urban Population: 44% of total population
Comparative Size: slightly smaller than Massachusetts
Gross Domestic Product (per capita): $8,200 (142nd in the world)
Gross Domestic Product (by sector): agriculture 13.1%, industry 16.0%, services 70.9%
Government: parliamentary democracy and a Commonwealth realm
Languages: English 62.9% (official), Spanish 56.6%, Creole 44.6%, Maya 10.5%, German 3.2%, Garifuna 2.9%, other 1.8%, unknown 0.3%, none 0.2% (cannot speak)

SOCIAL PROGRESS SNAPSHOT

Foundations of Well-being: 65.56 (–.89 below 66.45 world average)
(Not all scores computed due to data gaps in statistical sources.)

Belize was the site of several Mayan city-states until the end of the first millennium AD. The British and Spanish disputed the region in the 17th and 18th centuries; it became the colony of British Honduras in 1854. Like Canada, as well as the Caribbean countries of Barbados and the Bahamas, it is one of 16 Commonwealth realms, or members of the Commonwealth of Nations, with Britain's Queen Elizabeth II as the constitutional monarch. Territorial disputes between the UK and Guatemala delayed Belize's independence until 1981. Guatemala refused to recognize Belize until 1992, and the two countries still dispute borders. Tourism has become the mainstay of the economy.

A zoo director teaches students about wildlife in Belize City, Belize.

Follow the index every year at socialprogressimperative.org.
Quick Stats from CIA World Factbook.

CENTRAL AMERICAN AND CARIBBEAN COUNTRIES AT A GLANCE   **65**

Costa Rica

QUICK STATS
Population: 4,814,144
Urban Population: 76.8% of total population
Comparative Size: slightly smaller than West Virginia
Gross Domestic Product (per capita): $14,900 (104th in the world)
Gross Domestic Product (by sector): agriculture 6%, industry 20.5%, services 73.4%
Government: democratic republic
Languages: Spanish (official), English

SOCIAL PROGRESS SNAPSHOT
Social Progress Index: 77.88 (+16.88 above 61.00 world average)
Basic Human Needs: 84.22 (+15.89 above 68.33 world average)
Foundations of Well-being: 78.83 (+12.38 above 66.45 world average)
Opportunity: 70.59 (+22.36 above 48.23 world average)

Early attempts to colonize Costa Rica were unsuccessful due to disease from mosquito-infested swamps, brutal heat, resistance by natives, and pirate raids. A permanent settlement was eventually established in the central highlands in 1563. In 1821 Costa Rica was among several provinces that declared independence from Spain. Two years later, Costa Rica proclaimed its own sovereignty. Costa Rica has strong technology and tourism industries, in addition to a large agricultural sector.

Cuba

QUICK STATS
Population: 11,031,433
Urban Population: 77.1 percent of total population
Comparative Size: slightly smaller than Pennsylvania
Gross Domestic Product (per capita): $10,200 (131st in the world)
Gross Domestic Product (by sector): agriculture 3.8%, industry 14.3%, services 81.9%
Government: Communist state
Language: Spanish (official)

SOCIAL PROGRESS SNAPSHOT
Social Progress Index: 60.83 (–.17 below 61.00 world average)
Basic Human Needs: 80.08 (+11.75 above 68.33 world average)
Foundations of Well-being: 60.51 (–5.94 below 66.45 world average)
Opportunity: 41.90 (–6.33 below 48.23 world average)

The native population of Cuba declined after European discovery in 1492 and during Spanish colonization over the next several centuries. Large numbers of African slaves were imported to work coffee and sugar plantations, and Havana became the launching point for treasure fleets bound for Spain from Mexico and Peru. US intervention during the Spanish-American War in 1898 helped the Cubans overthrow Spanish rule. The United States cut diplomatic relations with Cuba in 1961 and did not reestablish them until 2015.

DOMINICAN REPUBLIC

QUICK STATS

Population: 10,478,756
Urban Population: 79% of total population
Comparative Size: slightly more than twice the size of New Hampshire
Gross Domestic Product (per capita): $13,000 (114th in the world)
Gross Domestic Product (by sector): agriculture 6.3%, industry 32.1%, services 61.6%
Government: democratic republic
Language: Spanish (official)

SOCIAL PROGRESS SNAPSHOT

Social Progress Index: 62.47 (+1.47 above 61.00 world average)
Basic Human Needs: 64.80 (–3.53 below 68.33 world average)
Foundations of Well-being: 71.95 (+5.50 above 66.45 world average)
Opportunity: 50.65 (+2.42 above 48.23 world average)

Columbus claimed Hispaniola Island in 1492. In 1697 Spain recognized French dominion over the western third of the island, which in 1804 became Haiti. The remainder of the island sought independence in 1821 but was conquered by the Haitians for 22 years; it finally attained independence as the Dominican Republic in 1844. In 1861 the Dominicans voluntarily returned to the Spanish Empire but two years later launched a war that restored independence in 1865.

EL SALVADOR

QUICK STATS

Population: 6,141,350
Urban Population: 66.7% of total population
Comparative Size: about the same size as New Jersey
Gross Domestic Product (per capita): $8,000 (143rd in the world)
Gross Domestic Product (by sector): agriculture 10%, industry 25.1%, services 64.9%
Government: republic
Languages: Spanish (official), Nahua (among some indigenous groups)

SOCIAL PROGRESS SNAPSHOT

Social Progress Index: 64.31 (+3.31 above 61.00 world average)
Basic Human Needs: 68.38 (+.05 above 68.33 world average)
Foundations of Well-being: 68.81 (+2.36 above 66.45 world average)
Opportunity: 55.75 (+7.52 above 48.23 world average)

El Salvador achieved independence from Spain in 1821 and from the Central American Federation in 1839. A 12-year civil war, which cost about 75,000 lives, was brought to a close in 1992 when the government and leftist rebels signed a treaty that provided for military and political reforms.

GUATEMALA

QUICK STATS
Population: 14,918,999
Urban Population: 51.6% of total population
Comparative Size: slightly smaller than Pennsylvania
Gross Domestic Product (per capita): $7,500 (151st in the world)
Gross Domestic Product (by sector): agriculture 13.3%, industry 23.5%, services 63.2%
Government: constitutional democratic republic
Languages: Spanish (official) 60%, indigenous languages 40%

SOCIAL PROGRESS SNAPSHOT
Social Progress Index: 62.19 (+1.19 above 61.00 world average)
Basic Human Needs: 69.32 (+.99 above 68.33 world average)
Foundations of Well-being: 68.96 (+2.51 above 66.45 world average)
Opportunity: 48.29 (+.06 above 48.23 world average)

The Maya civilization flourished in Guatemala and surrounding regions during the first millennium AD. After almost three centuries as a Spanish colony, Guatemala won its independence in 1821. During the second half of the 20th century, it experienced a variety of governments and a 36-year war. In 1996 the government signed a peace agreement ending the internal conflict, which had left more than 200,000 dead and created about one million refugees.

HAITI

QUICK STATS
Population: 10,110,019
Urban Population: 58.6% of total population
Comparative Size: slightly smaller than Maryland
Gross Domestic Product (per capita): $1,800 (207th in the world)
Gross Domestic Product (by sector): agriculture 24.7%, industry 20%, services 55.3%
Government: republic
Languages: French (official), Creole (official)

SOCIAL PROGRESS SNAPSHOT
Basic Human Needs: 36.02 (−32.31 below 68.33 world average)
Foundations of Well-being: not available
Opportunity: 36.89 (−11.34 below 48.23 world average)
(Not all scores computed due to data gaps in statistical sources.)

Hispaniola Island was claimed by Columbus in 1492. Its native Taino people were virtually annihilated by Spanish settlers within 25 years. In 1697 Spain ceded to the French the western third of the island, which later became Haiti. The French colony became one of the wealthiest in the Caribbean through the importation of African slaves. In the late 18th century, Haiti's nearly half million slaves revolted, and Haiti became the first postcolonial black-led nation in 1804.

HONDURAS

QUICK STATS

Population: 8,746,673
Urban Population: 54.7% of total population
Comparative Size: slightly larger than Tennessee
Gross Domestic Product (per capita): $4,700 (173rd in the world)
Gross Domestic Product (by sector): agriculture 14.0%, industry 27.4%, services 58.7%
Government: democratic constitutional republic
Languages: Spanish (official), indigenous dialects

SOCIAL PROGRESS SNAPSHOT

Social Progress Index: 61.44 (+.44 above 61.00 world average)
Basic Human Needs: 65.29 (–3.04 below 68.33 world average)
Foundations of Well-being: 72.71 (+6.26 above 66.45 world average)
Opportunity: 46.32 (–1.91 below 48.23 world average)

Once part of Spain's vast empire, Honduras became independent in 1821. After 25 years of mostly military rule, a freely elected civilian government came to power in 1982. During the 1980s, Honduras proved a haven for those fighting the Marxist Nicaraguan government and an ally to Salvadoran government forces fighting leftist guerrillas. The country was devastated by Hurricane Mitch in 1998, which killed thousands and caused billions of dollars of damage.

JAMAICA

QUICK STATS

Population: 2,950,210
Urban Population: 54.8% of total population
Comparative Size: slightly smaller than Connecticut
Gross Domestic Product (per capita): $8,600 (136th in the world)
Gross Domestic Product (by sector): agriculture 6.9%, industry 21.1%, services 72%
Government: constitutional parliamentary democracy and a Commonwealth realm
Languages: English, English patois

SOCIAL PROGRESS SNAPSHOT

Social Progress Index: 69.83 (+8.83 above 61.00 world average)
Basic Human Needs: 70.52 (+2.19 above 68.33 world average)
Foundations of Well-being: 72.84 (+6.39 above 66.45 world average)
Opportunity: 66.14 (+17.91 above 48.23 world average)

Columbus discovered Jamaica in 1494. It was settled by the Spanish in the early 1500s. Native people were killed by disease and violence and replaced with African slaves. Britain seized Jamaica in 1655 and established a plantation economy. Abolition of slavery in 1834 freed 750,000 slaves. Jamaica gained independence in 1962. Crime, drug trafficking, and poverty pose challenges today, but many rural and resort areas remain relatively safe and contribute substantially to the economy.

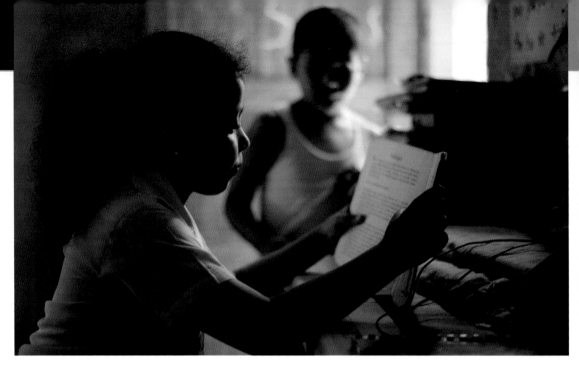

Seven-year-old student Maria Fernanda reads a book for a reading club at school while her brother watches at her family's home in the village of San Francisco in the municipality of Nindiri, Nicaragua.

NICARAGUA

QUICK STATS

Population: 5,907,881
Urban Population: 58.8% of total population
Comparative Size: slightly larger than Pennsylvania; slightly smaller than New York
Gross Domestic Product (per capita): $4,700 (172nd in the world)
Gross Domestic Product (by sector): agriculture 14.9%, industry 28.8%, services 56.4%
Government: republic
Languages: Spanish (official) 95.3%, Miskito 2.2%, Mestizo 2%, other 0.5%

SOCIAL PROGRESS SNAPSHOT

Social Progress Index: 62.20 (+1.20 above 61.00 world average)
Basic Human Needs: 65.87 (–2.46 below 68.33 world average)
Foundations of Well-being: 72.17 (+5.72 above 66.45 world average)
Opportunity: 48.58 (+.35 above 48.23 world average)

Nicaragua was settled as a Spanish colony in the early 16th century. Independence was declared in 1821, and the country became independent in 1838. Britain occupied the Caribbean coast in the first half of the 19th century but gradually ceded control. Violent opposition to government corruption spread in 1978 and resulted in a short-lived civil war that brought the Marxist Sandinista guerrillas to power in 1979.

PANAMA

QUICK STATS
Population: 3,657,024
Urban Population: 66.6% of total population
Comparative Size: slightly smaller than South Carolina
Gross Domestic Product (per capita): $19,500 (82nd in the world)
Gross Domestic Product (by sector): agriculture 2.9%, industry 14.1%, services 83%
Government: constitutional democracy
Languages: Spanish (official), indigenous languages (including Ngabe, Bugle, Kuna, Embera, Wounaan, Naso Tjerdi, and Bri Bri)

SOCIAL PROGRESS SNAPSHOT
Social Progress Index: 71.79 (+10.79 above 61.00 world average)
Basic Human Needs: 75.91 (+7.58 above 68.33 world average)
Foundations of Well-being: 77.55 (+11.10 above 66.45 world average)
Opportunity: 61.90 (+13.67 above 48.23 world average)

Settled by the Spanish in the 1500s, Panama broke with Spain in 1821 and joined the Republic of Gran Colombia. When Gran Colombia dissolved in 1830, Panama remained part of Colombia. With US backing, Panama seceded from Colombia in 1903 and signed a treaty allowing the US to construct the Panama Canal, which was built between 1904 and 1914. The canal, surrounding areas, and US bases were transferred to Panama by the end of 1999.

TRINIDAD AND TOBAGO

QUICK STATS
Population: 1,222,363
Urban Population: 8.4% of total population
Comparative Size: slightly smaller than Delaware
Gross Domestic Product (per capita): $32,100 (43rd in the world)
Gross Domestic Product (by sector): agriculture 0.5%, industry 15.2%, services 84.3%
Government: parliamentary democracy
Languages: English (official), Caribbean Hindustani (a dialect of Hindi), French, Spanish, Chinese

SOCIAL PROGRESS SNAPSHOT
Basic Human Needs: 75.18 (+6.85 above 68.33 world average)
Foundations of Well-being: not available
Opportunity: 63.83 (+15.60 above 48.23 world average)
(Not all scores computed due to data gaps in statistical sources.)

First colonized by the Spanish, the islands came under British control in the early 19th century. The islands' sugar industry was hurt by the emancipation of the slaves in 1834. Manpower was replaced with contract laborers from India between 1845 and 1917. Trinidad and Tobago became independent in 1962. The country is one of the most prosperous in the Caribbean primarily from petroleum and natural gas production and processing. Tourism in Tobago is growing.

Conclusion

In this volume, you've seen that wealthier countries often have higher social progress scores but that a better economy does not guarantee more social progress. You've also seen that a high score doesn't always mean social progress for everyone. Racial and ethnic minorities, immigrants, and rural populations often don't have the same access to food, housing, medical care, and education that other groups enjoy. Poverty and discrimination can deny people their basic rights and limit their access to the courts.

Ranking the scores revealed relative strengths and weaknesses in each country based on the size of its economy. Looking at relative weaknesses is important because countries can see where others with similar resources are doing a better job, which may give them ideas or motivation to make changes. For example, the Dominican Republic, Haiti, and Trinidad and Tobago all have work to do in providing for Basic Human Needs. Belize has room to grow in the Foundations of Well-being category, especially in the categories of Ecosystem Sustainability and Access to Information and Communications. Guatemala needs to improve in Access to Basic Knowledge. In the Opportunity category, the Dominican Republic and Trinidad and Tobago should consider how to improve Access to Advanced Education, and Cuba could consider changes that would improve Personal Freedom and Choice and Personal Rights.

Trinidad and Tobago is an example of a country that is making a commitment to using social progress measures to guide its social development. The only high-income country in the Caribbean, Trinidad and Tobago's scores in the Basic Human Needs categories are relatively weak compared to its economic equals, such as Greece, New Zealand, and Portugal. As a result,

Trinidad and Tobago has committed to measuring social progress inside the country using the SPI model. It plans to create a team of government, business, and civil society organizations to measure, and then improve, social progress in the country. As more countries follow the example of Trinidad and Tobago, the world will see social progress increase in every measure.

If Central America and the Caribbean were combined into a single country, a Social Progress Snapshot like those in Chapter 4 could be calculated by averaging the SPI scores of these two regions. Using simple averages, the Central America and the Caribbean's Snapshot might look like this:

SOCIAL PROGRESS SNAPSHOT FOR CENTRAL AMERICA AND THE CARIBBEAN

Social Progress Index: 65.88 (+1.49 above 64.39 world average)
Basic Human Needs: 69.26 (−1.56 below above 70.82 world average)
Foundations of Well-being: 70.99 (+3.31 above 67.68 world average)
Opportunity: 53.12 (+1.09 above 52.03 world average)

Although there is much work to be done, the situation in many countries has improved in recent years. The Social Progress Imperative found that, as a group, Central American and Caribbean countries have more balanced social progress scores across the three categories of Basic Human Needs, Foundations of Well-being, and Opportunity than other world regions have. It noted, "At least in part, this balance reflects some common investments across Latin America in social progress. Government and civil society have worked to largely eradicate extreme hunger or homelessness, and provide access to

Citizens march for International Women's Day in San Jose, Costa Rica.

primary and secondary education. And, relative to many other areas of the world, there has been a significant shift toward choices enhancing Opportunity, including a commitment to personal rights as well as broad tolerance."

For more than 70 years, gross domestic product (GDP) has been the main tool used to measure and evaluate a country's success, but the things people really need and care about aren't measured by GDP. Measures of basic human needs, medical care, education, tolerance, rights, and freedoms paint a more accurate picture of a country's strengths and weaknesses that citizens and their leaders can use to guide their next steps toward improved social progress. Today, the work of the Social Progress Imperative is helping us understand that real success must consider social progress and that social progress must benefit everyone.

Series Glossary

Anemia: a condition in which the blood doesn't have enough healthy red blood cells, most often caused by not having enough iron

Aquifer: an underground layer of water-bearing permeable rock, from which groundwater can be extracted using a water well

Asylum: protection granted by a nation to someone who has left their native country as a political refugee

Basic human needs: the things people need to stay alive: clean water, sanitation, food, shelter, basic medical care, safety

Biodiversity: the variety of life that is absolutely essential to the health of different ecosystems

Carbon dioxide (CO_2): a greenhouse gas that contributes to global warming and climate change

Censorship: the practice of officially examining books, movies, and other media and art, and suppressing unacceptable parts

Child mortality rate: the number of children that die before their fifth birthday for every 1,000 babies born alive

Communicable diseases: medical conditions spread by airborne viruses or bacteria or through bodily fluids such as malaria, tuberculosis, and HIV/AIDS; also called **infectious diseases;** differ from **noncommunicable diseases**, medical conditions not caused by infection and requiring long-term treatment such as diabetes or heart disease

Contraception: any form of birth control used to prevent pregnancy

Corruption: the dishonest behavior by people in positions of power for their own benefit

Deforestation: the clearing of trees, transforming a forest into cleared land

Desalination: a process that removes minerals (including salt) from ocean water

Discrimination: the unjust or prejudicial treatment of different categories of people, especially on the grounds of race, age, or sex

Ecosystem: a biological community of interacting organisms and their physical environment

Ecosystem sustainability: when we care for resources like clean air, water, plants, and animals so that they will be available to future generations

Emissions: the production and discharge of something, especially gas or radiation

Ethnicities: social groups that have a common national or cultural tradition

Extremism: the holding of extreme political or religious views; fanaticism

Famine: a widespread scarcity of food that results in malnutrition and starvation on a large scale

Food desert: a neighborhood or community with no walking access to affordable, nutritious food

Food security: having enough to eat at all times

Greenhouse gas emissions: any of the atmospheric gases that contribute to the greenhouse effect by absorbing infrared radiation produced by solar warming of the earth's surface. They include carbon dioxide (CO_2), methane (CH_4), nitrous oxide (NO_2), and water vapor.

Gross domestic product (GDP): the total value of all products and services created in a country during a year

GDP per capita (per person): the gross domestic product divided by the number of people in the country. For example, if the GDP for a country is one hundred million dollars ($100,000,000) and the population is one million people (1,000,000), then the GDP per capita (value created per person) is $100.

Habitat: environment for a plant or animal, including climate, food, water, and shelter

Incarceration: the condition of being imprisoned

Income inequality: when the wealth of a country is spread very unevenly among the population

Indigenous people: culturally distinct groups with long-standing ties to the land in a specific area

Inflation: when the same amount money buys less from one day to the next. Just because things cost more does not mean that people have more money. Low-income people trapped in a high inflation economy can quickly find themselves unable to purchase even the basics like food.

Infrastructure: permanent features required for an economy to operate such as transportation routes and electric grids; also systems such as education and courts

Latrine: a communal outdoor toilet, such as a trench dug in the ground

Literate: able to read and write

Malnutrition: lack of proper nutrition, caused by not having enough to eat, not eating enough of the right things, or being unable to use the food that one does eat

Maternal mortality rate: the number of pregnant women who die for every 100,000 births.

Natural resources: industrial materials and assets provided by nature such as metal deposits, timber, and water

Nongovernmental organization (NGO): a nonprofit, voluntary citizens' group organized on a local, national, or international level. Examples include organizations that support human rights, advocate for political participation, and work for improved health care.

Parliament: a group of people who are responsible for making the laws in some kinds of government

Prejudice: an opinion that isn't based on facts or reason

Preventive care: health care that helps an individual avoid illness

Primary school: includes grades 1–6 (also known as elementary school); precedes **secondary** and **tertiary education**, schooling beyond the primary grades; secondary generally corresponds to high school, and tertiary generally means college-level

Privatization: the transfer of ownership, property, or business from the government to the private sector (the part of the national economy that is not under direct government control)

Sanitation: conditions relating to public health, especially the provision of clean drinking water and adequate sewage disposal

Stereotypes: are common beliefs about the nature of the members of a specific group that are based on limited experience or incorrect information

Subsistence agriculture: a system of farming that supplies the needs of the farm family without generating any surplus for sale

Surface water: the water found above ground in streams, lakes, and rivers

Tolerance: a fair, objective, and permissive attitude toward those whose opinions, beliefs, practices, racial or ethnic origins, and so on differ from one's own

Trafficking: dealing or trading in something illegal

Transparency: means that the government operates in a way that is visible to and understood by the public

Universal health care: a system in which every person in a country has access to doctors and hospitals

Urbanization: the process by which towns and cities are formed and become larger as more and more people begin living and working in central areas

Well-being: the feeling people have when they are healthy, comfortable, and happy

Whistleblower: someone who reveals private information about the illegal activities of a person or organization

Index

basic human needs, 12, 15-26, 72, 73, 74

biodiversity and habitat, 42-43

climate change, 42, 43, 44

corruption, 47, 50, 52, 53

crime, 24, 25, 26, 40, 52

discrimination, 55, 56, 57, 72

disease, 15, 18, 22, 32, 55

drugs, 11, 24, 25

ecosystems, 32, 33, 41, 72

education, 12, 31, 34, 36, 47, 51, 53, 58, 72, 74

education, higher, 47, 48, 72

electricity, 16, 24

food, 12, 15, 16, 18, 19, 21, 42, 72

freedom, 12, 38, 39, 40, 47, 49, 50, 52, 60, 72, 74

information and communications, access to, 32, 33, 38-40, 72

    Internet, 32, 38, 39, 40

foundations of well-being, 12, 31-45, 72, 73

garbage, 19

government, 11, 32, 35, 36, 39, 40, 47, 51, 52, 57, 60, 61, 62, 68, 73

greenhouse gas emissions, 41, 44

health, 16, 18, 21, 23, 31, 32, 33, 36, 38

    health care, 12, 21, 36, 37

    infant mortality, 18, 21, 22, 25

    maternal health, 21, 22

housing, 16, 20, 24, 53, 57, 72

immigrants, 53, 55, 57, 72

income, 13, 15, 17, 18, 22, 23, 26, 36, 39, 49, 58, 72

literacy, 31, 35, 36

medical care, 12, 15, 16, 18, 19, 22, 72, 73,

minorities, 53, 55, 72

nutrition, 16, 17, 18, 19, 20

opportunity, 12, 34, 47-62, 72, 73, 74

pollution, 24, 42, 43

poverty, 11, 17, 18, 25, 34, 37, 57, 62, 72

religion, 47, 50, 54, 57

rights, 12, 15, 39, 46, 47, 49, 57, 59, 61, 62, 72, 74

safety, 16, 17, 18, 24, 26, 40, 54

sanitation, 15, 16, 17, 18, 19, 20, 22, 23

shelter, 12, 15, 16, 17, 19, 23, 24

social progress, in Central America and the Caribbean (overview), 11

tolerance, 47, 53, 54, 57, 58, 74

    for homosexuals, 58

    for immigrants, 57

unemployment, 21

violence, 11, 16, 24, 25, 40, 55

vote, 61

water, 12, 15, 16, 17, 18, 19, 20, 22, 23, 41, 42, 44, 45

wealth, 13, 18, 22, 26, 72

RESOURCES

Continue exploring the world of development through this assortment of online and print resources. Follow links, stay organized, and maintain a critical perspective. Also, seek out news sources from outside the country in which you live.

Websites

Social Progress Imperative: socialprogressimperative.org

United Nations—Human Development Indicators: hdr.undp.org/en/countries and Sustainable Development Goals: un.org/sustainabledevelopment/sustainable-development-goals

World Bank—World Development Indicators: data.worldbank.org/data-catalog/world-development-indicators

World Health Organization—country statistics: who.int/gho/countries/en

U.S. State Department—human rights tracking site: humanrights.gov/dyn/countries.html

Oxfam International: oxfam.org/en

Amnesty International: amnesty.org/en

Human Rights Watch: hrw.org

Reporters without Borders: en.rsf.org

CIA—The World Factbook: cia.gov/library/publications/the-world-factbook

Books

Literary and classics

The Good Earth, Pearl S. Buck

Grapes of Wrath, John Steinbeck

The Jungle, Upton Sinclair

Nonfiction—historical/classic

Angela's Ashes, Frank McCourt

Lakota Woman, Mary Crow Dog with Richard Erdoes

Orientalism, Edward Said

Silent Spring, Rachel Carson

The Souls of Black Folk, W.E.B. Du Bois

Nonfiction: development and policy—presenting a range of views

Behind the Beautiful Forevers: Life, Death, and Hope in a Mumbai Undercity, Katherine Boo

The Bottom Billion: Why the Poorest Countries Are Failing and What Can Be Done About It, Paul Collier

The End of Poverty, Jeffrey D. Sachs

For the Common Good: Redirecting the Economy toward Community, the Environment, and a Sustainable Future, Herman E. Daly

I Am Malala: The Girl Who Stood Up for Education and Was Shot by the Taliban, Malala Yousafzai and Christina Lamb

The Life You Can Save: Acting Now to End World Poverty, Peter Singer

Mismeasuring Our Lives: Why GDP Doesn't Add Up, Joseph E. Stiglitz, Amartya Sen, and Jean-Paul Fitoussi

Rachel and Her Children: Homeless Families in America, Jonathan Kozol

The White Man's Burden: Why the West's Efforts to Aid the Rest Have Done So Much Ill and So Little Good, William Easterly

Foreword writer Michael Green is an economist, author, and cofounder of the Social Progressive Imperative. A UK native and graduate of Oxford University, Green has worked in aid and development for the British government and taught economics at Warsaw University.

Author Judy Boyd has designed and developed self-study workbooks, instructor-led courses, and online learning modules to teach language, technology, and mapping. She holds a B.S. in cartography and an M.S. in interactive telecommunications. She lives in Santa Fe, New Mexico, where she works as a freelance writer and watercolor artist.